ED EMBERLEY'S FINGERPRINT DRAWING BOOK

LITTLE, BROWN AND COMPANY

BOSTON   NEW YORK   LONDON

This book shows how to make pictures using your fingerprints and a few scribbles, dots, and lines....

Simple step-by-step instructions show you how.

This row shows what to draw.

This row shows where to put it.

1. Press ink.　　2. Press paper.　　3. Draw.

ABOUT PRINTERS

Your finger will do for a start.

For cleaner hands and a greater choice of sizes you can make your own stampers.

An artist's gum-rubber eraser is easy to carve and fun to use.

So are assorted veggies such as carrots or potatoes.

For a very special gift, for yourself or someone else, you can have a custom rubber stamp made from your fingerprint. Inquire at any printer or office-supply store.

ABOUT INK PADS

There are a number of different kinds of ink pads you can use. Office stamp pads are inexpensive and can be found in places that sell office supplies. Colors are limited to red, blue, black, and sometimes green.

CAUTION: Since pads are made for adult office use, the ink is not necessarily nontoxic or washable.

Craft stamp pads are harder to find and usually more expensive than standard office ink pads. They can be found in many places that sell arts and crafts supplies. They come in lots of bright colors and are available washable and nontoxic.

You could also try making your own ink pads from cloth or paper towels and whatever coloring you have on hand. This is the least expensive way to go, but it will take some experimentation to get just the right combination of paint and pad.

Of course, you are not limited to stamping or printing. Cut paper, fabric, stencils, blobs of paint, lumps of clay—anything with which you can make a roundish shape will work using these instructions.

ABOUT MARKERS

A pencil will do for a start.

After that, which marker you choose will depend on the size of your print and the ink used.

For this book I used a colored pencil for the colored lines and a fine-point fiber-tip pen for the black lines. Both were found in the stationery section of my local drugstore.

ODDS AND ENDS

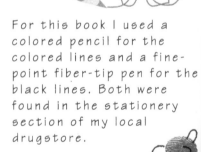

You will also need paper to print on and a table to work on; plastic or newspapers to protect the table; work clothes to protect the artist; and paper towels and soap and water for cleaning up.

There are billions of fingerprints in the world.
No two have ever been found that are just alike.
There never has been and there never will be fingerprints just like yours.
That makes your fingerprints very special.

THIS AND THAT
CIRCLES AND OVALS

I used two kinds of fingerprints to make this book. Ovals and circles.

The ovals were made by using my whole fingertip.

The circles were made by using just the very tip of my finger.

For carrot printing, use a straight cut for circles, and an angled cut for ovals.

Adult supervision is advised for ALL cutting.

ONE OR MANY

Sometimes when I make fingerprint pictures, I like to use just one color at a time because it's quick and easy.

Sometimes I use lots of colors and lots of fingers.

When I want to change colors, I dip my finger in a glass of water and then wipe it off on a stack of paper towels.
That keeps my ink pads bright and clean.

Rinse.   Wipe.

EXTRA FOR EXPERTS
HALF PRINTS

In a few places in this book, I used half prints. Here's how I made them.

1. Place paper shield. 2. Print half on, half off paper shield. 3. Remove paper shield. 4. Draw.

1. Print. 2. Cover with paper shield. 3. Print half on, half off paper shield.

4. Remove paper shield. 5. Draw. Too complicated? Use just one color.

Half circles are just right for making watermelons, monkeys, and other things. Can you find the half prints in these two things?

CONTINUED ON LAST PAGE

THE GARDEN

FLOWER

SNAIL

FROG

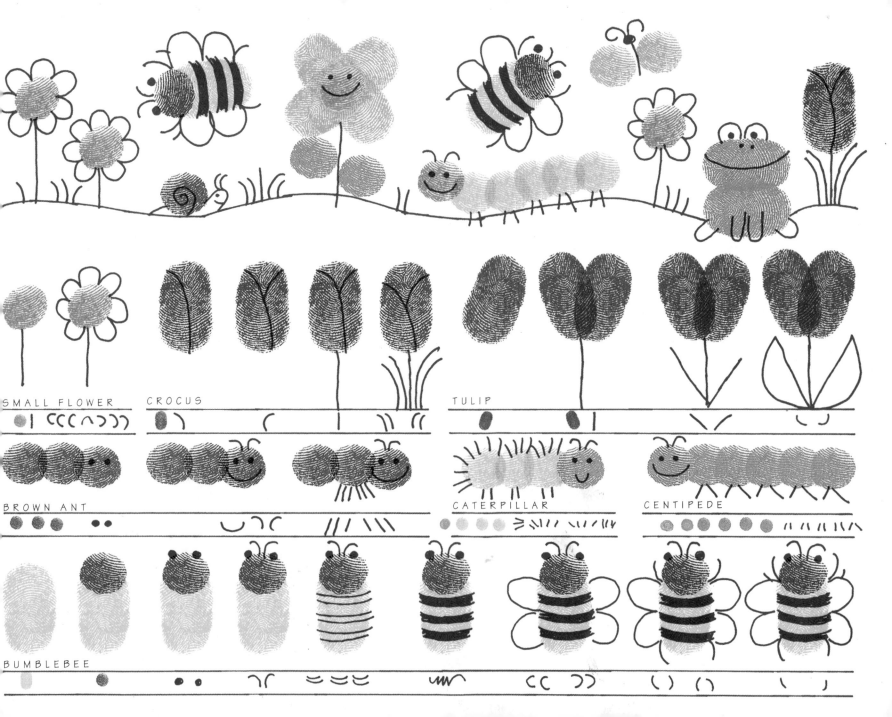

SMALL FLOWER

CROCUS

TULIP

BROWN ANT

CATERPILLAR

CENTIPEDE

BUMBLEBEE

THE POND

TURTLE

DUCK

POLLYWOG

BUTTERFLY

SWIMMING FROG

BIG FISH

LITTLE FISH

FINGERLINGS

I ALSO CALL THESE MY
TEENY TINIES. I USE A
DIFFERENT FINGERTIP FOR
EACH COLOR.

SPRING

SUMMER

RABBIT

MOUSE

OWL

FROG

DOG

BEAVER

FALL

FALL

WINTER

SITTING CAT

BIRD

STANDING

Make face same
as sitting cat.

FLYING

RUNNING

Make face same
as sitting cat.

PECKING

ANIMALS

ELEPHANT

BABY ELEPHANT

LION

MORE ANIMALS

RACCOON

PIG

BEAVER

DOG

CAT

SMALL BULLDOG

MOUSE

BIG BULLDOG

BIRDS

BABY BIRDS IN NEST

BIRD EATING WORM

BIRD FRONT VIEW

BIRD BACK VIEW

BIRD FLYING

BIRD SINGING

BIRD EATING

BIRD WALKING

BEAN BUDDIES

I THINK FINGERPRINTS LOOK LIKE LITTLE BEANS. I LIKE TO USE THESE LITTLE "FINGER BEANS" TO MAKE ALL DIFFERENT KINDS OF LITTLE BEAN BUDDIES.

BASIC

PEA BEAN BUDDY

BAKED BEAN BUDDY

LIMA BEAN BUDDY

JELLY BEAN BUDDY

SPEAKING   HI!

POINTING   LOOK

YAWNING   HO HUM

CELEBRATING   HOORAY.

GRUMBLING   HRUMPH

WONDERING

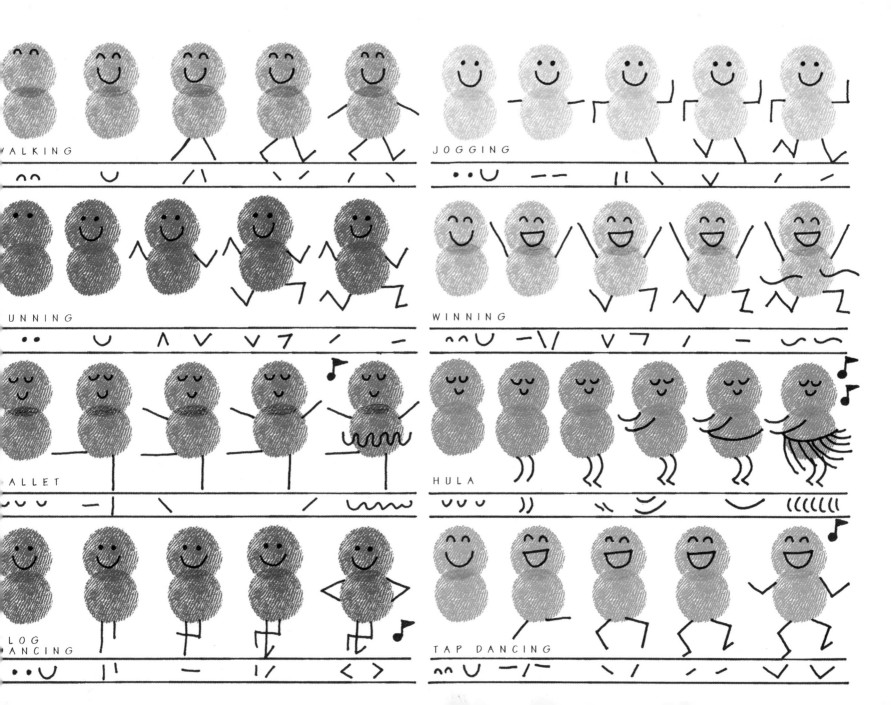

WALKING

JOGGING

UNNING

WINNING

ALLET

HULA

LOG
ANCING

TAP DANCING

LITTLE CLOWN

NAPOLEON

SAILOR

QUEEN

KING

PRINCE

OWBOY

COWGIRL   BANDIT

IRATE

SUPERPERSON

EVIL VILLAIN

EV

FEELINGS

HAPPY

VERY HAPPY

VERY VERY HAPPY

SNOOTY

SAD

VERY SAD

VERY VERY SAD

UPSET

ANGRY

VERY ANGRY

VERY VERY ANGRY

SLY (MISCHIEVOUS)

SHY (EMBARRASSED)

SUSPICIOUS

HURTING

OUC
OUCH

MUSIC

HUMMING

MMM

WHISTLING

SINGING

SINGERS

SKIPPING ROPE

BICYCLING

SKATEBOARDING

ROLLER-SKATING

APRIL SHOWERS

FISHING

HIKING

KITES

SUMMER FUN

CHASING BUTTERFLIES

SWIMMING

SURFING

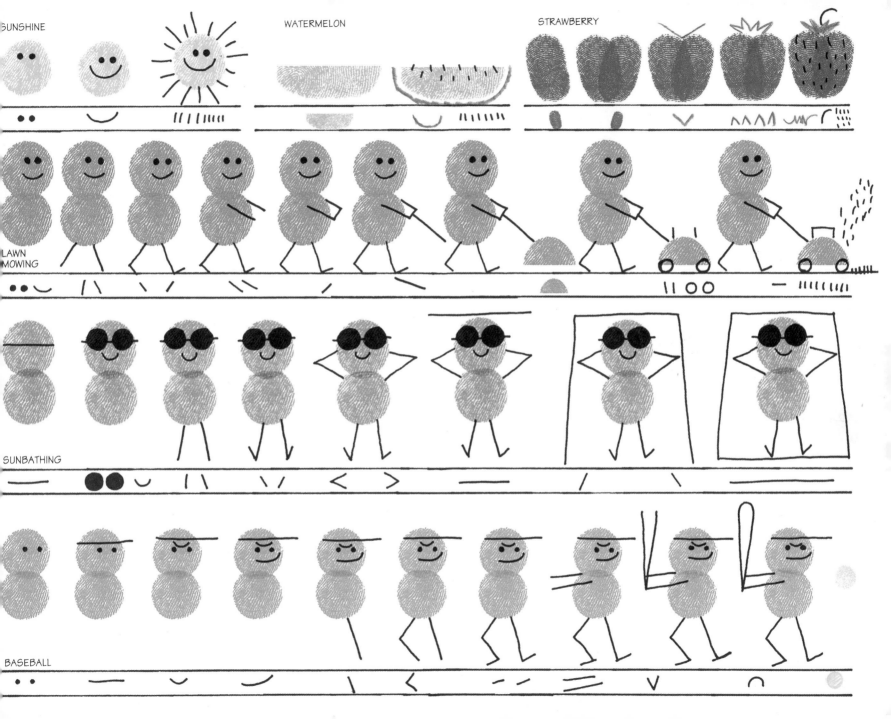

SUNSHINE

WATERMELON

STRAWBERRY

LAWN MOWING

SUNBATHING

BASEBALL

FALL
FUN

APPLE

PEAR

YELLOW APPLE

HAPPY GREEN APPLE

GRAPES

FARMING

LACROSSE

SOCCER

FOOTBALL

SPORTS FAN

CHEERLEADER

BASKETBALL

WINTER FUN

PENGUIN FRONT VIEW

PENGUIN SIDE VIEW

SNOWPERSON

SKIING

SKATING

HOCKEY

HOLIDAYS

EASTER BUNNY

EASTER EGG

CHOCOLATE EGG

CHICK

VALENTINE

SHAMROCK

LEPRECHAUN

PILGRIM

TURKEY

PILGRIM

INDIAN

HALLOWEEN

WITCH

FLYING WITCH

JACK-O-LANTERN

BAT

SKELETON

OWL

SPIDER

CAT

JINGLE   JINGLE

JINGLE

LAND SEA AND AIR

CAR

SUBMARINE

BLIMP

HELICOPTER

TRAIN

ENGINE

COAL CAR

PASSENGER CAR

FREIGHT CAR

RAINBOW CLOWN

COO COO

FESTER

LULU

RAINBOW DRAGON

LION

LION FACE

LION MANE

RAINBOW LIONS

SKETCH BOOK

HERE ARE SOME FINGERPRINT THINGS I COULD NOT FIT INTO THIS BOOK. CAN YOU FIGURE OUT HOW I MADE THEM?

NOSES

HAIR

EYES
AND
EARS

HATS

ADVANCED FINGER-PRINTING

FOR THE ADVENTUROUS—
JUST A FEW OTHER WAYS TO COMBINE PRINTS,
COLORS, SIMPLE LINES, AND SOME
IMAGINATION TO MAKE PICTURES.
THERE ARE LOTS LEFT FOR YOU TO DISCOVER.
HAPPY DISCOVERING!

SOMETHING VERY SPECIAL

The instructions in this book are meant to show a few ways to turn fingerprints into an owl or a cat or a dog, etc. Much has been left for you to explore and discover.

Just as no two fingerprints will ever look just alike, no two fingerprint pictures will ever look just alike. Fingerprints will be lighter or darker, lines will be thicker or thinner, colors will be different.

That means no other fingerprint pictures will look just like the ones in this book, or just like yours. That's what will make your pictures "something very special."

This is the way this book shows you how to make a fingerprint owl.

Here are some other "explorations."

Sometimes I like to use natural colors, sometimes I like to use imaginary colors.

Sometimes I like to use other fingerprints.

Sometimes I like to add a few extra lines.

Library of Congress Cataloging-in-Publication Data

Emberley, Ed.
[Fingerprint drawing book]
Ed Emberley's fingerprint drawing book—1st ed.
p. cm.
ISBN 0-316-23638-1 (HC) / ISBN 0-316-23319-6 (PB) /
ISBN 0-316-23213-0 (Hearth Song)
1. Fingerprints in art.   2. Drawing—Technique.   I. Title.

NC825.F55 E46 2001
741.2—dc21
00-031026